To Florence, with love, and appreciation for her friendship!

The Millers

February, 1982

The New Testament in Living Pictures

A Photo Guide to the New Testament

BY DAVID S. ALEXANDER

A Division of G/L Publications
Glendale, California, U.S.A.

Published in North America by
Regal Books Division, G/L Publications
Glendale, California 91209, U.S.A.

Copyright © 1972 Lion Publishing

Photographs and notes by
David S. Alexander

Scripture quotations from
The Living Bible, copyright 1971
by Tyndale House Publishers,
and used by permission.

ISBN 0-8307-0172-9
Library of Congress Catalog Card No. 72-85232

First edition September 1972
Second edition 1973
Third edition 1974

Printed in Great Britain by
Purnell and Sons Ltd, Paulton, U.K.

Introduction

Those who have been to the sites of the New Testament story, in Israel and Jordan, Greece and Turkey, will know the excitement of seeing the places where the events actually took place. It makes the Bible events come to life. It helps us understand the text of the New Testament afresh. The aim of this book is the same; to provide pictures which make the setting of the New Testament live for those who cannot visit the places themselves.

It often comes as a surprise to the visitor to the Middle East to find so many remains from New Testament times. There is no reason why there should be this surprise, for the Bible consists of documents which are at least as trustworthy historically as any ancient writings. But each year sees some new attack on the Bible's reliability (usually by people who do not want it to be true because they do not dare to face the challenge of its message). So it still comes as a confirmation to faith when people find its setting so obviously and accurately that of the Jewish, Roman and Hellenistic world which has left so many traces for us to see and admire.

In fact the person looking for New Testament sites often finds himself on the main tourist track. Places such as Ephesus in Western Turkey not only provide a marvelous aid to understanding the drama of the New Testament Acts and Epistles but are also among the main attractions of the area for those who have no prior interest in the Bible. This serves to underline the fact that the events of the New Testament which so determined the subsequent history, culture and hope of the civilized world took place at a unique time in history. Hebrew religion, Greek language and culture, Roman imperial administration made possible the immediate and widespread dissemination of the Christian good news. No wonder St Paul maintained that 'the time had fully come'. The time was ripe in a way which it has never been before or since.

The choice of pictures has been determined by the aim of the book. Thus some of the traditional sites have not been included, although they have been hallowed by centuries of devotion, because they no longer help us to imagine what it must have been like in New Testament times. The picture of a first-century tomb complete with rolling stone is quite simply more informative and more evocative than a picture of the church built on the traditional site of Jesus' burial. A photograph of the Roman pavement where Jesus actually stood trial before Pilate has been chosen as more suitable for this particular purpose than, say, one which shows the Stations of the Cross.

The aim of this book, then, is not only simple; it is practical. It is intended to help ordinary people understand the Bible all the better for seeing it against its background, and to remind them that it is not a fairy story to be grown out of, but the record of what actually happened over nineteen hundred years ago in Mediterranean towns and countryside which can still be seen.

The Bible is historical. But it is more than that. It is meant to take us beyond the background, which can be conjured up with the help of a book such as this, to the Person who is at the centre of the picture. He has not changed. He is alive today, and as relevant as when the message of his forgiveness, power and challenge revolutionized the ancient world. It is hoped that the stimulus of these photographs and brief accompanying comment will make many turn afresh to read the New Testament itself with a new confidence in its historicity and a new willingness to hear its message.

Michael Green
*St John's College,
Nottingham*

Contents

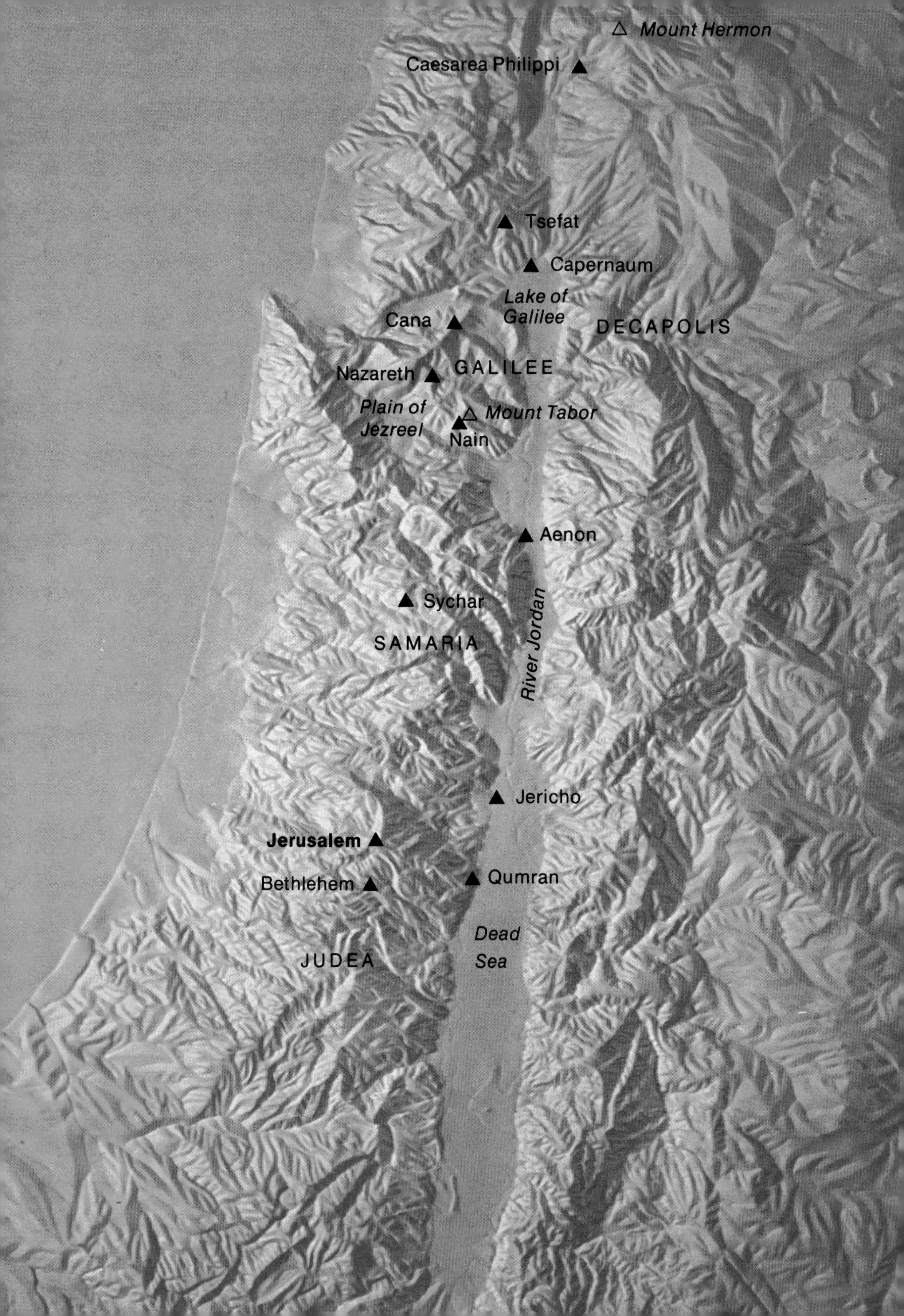

△ *Mount Hermon*

Caesarea Philippi ▲

▲ Tsefat

▲ Capernaum

Lake of Galilee

DECAPOLIS

Cana ▲

GALILEE

Nazareth ▲

Plain of Jezreel

△ *Mount Tabor*

Nain

▲ Aenon

River Jordan

▲ Sychar

SAMARIA

▲ Jericho

Jerusalem ▲

Bethlehem ▲

▲ Qumran

JUDEA

Dead Sea

PART ONE

The Life and Teaching of Jesus

Bethlehem

"About this time Caesar Augustus, the Roman Emperor, decreed that a census should be taken throughout the nation. . . . And because Joseph was a member of the royal line, he had to go to Bethlehem in Judea, King David's ancient home —journeying there from the Galilean village of Nazareth. He took with him Mary, his fiancée, who was obviously pregnant by this time. And while they were there, ·. . she gave birth to her first child, a son." Luke 2:1,4-7

Bethlehem stands on a ridge on the edge of the arid Judean desert, just south of Jerusalem. It is still surrounded by fields, with shepherds 'watching their flocks', as when Jesus was born. The Emperor Augustus was not to know that his decree would bring Joseph and Mary down to Bethlehem and so fulfil the prophet Micah's prediction that it would be from Bethlehem that a ruler would come 'who will govern my people Israel'.

Nazareth

"They returned home to Nazareth in Galilee. There the child became a strong, robust lad, and was known for wisdom beyond his years; and God poured out his blessings on him." Luke 2:39,40

Up the steep escarpment from the broad Plain of Jezreel, Nazareth lies cupped in the hills of Galilee, 1230 ft above sea level. Today Nazareth is a town with a sizeable population. But before it became the home of Jesus it was little known: it is not mentioned at all in the Old Testament. And though in New Testament times it was a busy town near the cross-roads of the Roman trade-routes, it still called forth the comment, 'Can anything good come out of Nazareth?' (John 1: 46).

Aenon near Salim

"He was baptizing at Aenon, near Salim, because there was plenty of water there." John 3:23

John the Baptist called people to turn from evil because 'the kingdom was at hand' — to shed their sin, like dead leaves and undergo the public 'washing' of baptism. In a country where water is sparse it was natural that his activity should be concentrated in the Jordan valley. Here the valley is already well below sea level, the heat and humidity producing sub-tropical vegetation.

The Jordan

"Then Jesus went from Galilee to the Jordan River to be baptized there by John. John didn't want to do it. 'This isn't proper,' he said. 'I am the one who needs to be baptized by you.' But Jesus said, 'Please do it, for I must do all that is right.' "
Matthew 3:13-15

The Jordan river rises at the foot of Mount Hermon on the border with Lebanon and Syria. After the Lake of Galilee it winds down through dense scrub and thickets towards the Dead Sea. It is not a large or pretentious river — in Old Testament days Naaman, the Syrian general, was quite indignant when Elisha told him to wash in it. But it was in this river that Jesus identified himself with the sins of his people as he allowed himself to be baptized.

"Then Jesus was led out into the wilderness by the Holy Spirit. . . . For forty days and forty nights he ate nothing . . . . Then Satan tempted him to get food by changing stones into . . . bread. 'It will prove you are the Son of God,' he said." Matthew 4:1-3

It was somewhere in this arid, stony desert south of Jerusalem that Jesus faced in advance the temptations that would threaten his whole ministry. He answered his tempter in words which go back to the testing of the children of Israel during their forty years in the wilderness centuries before, 'Man shall not live by bread alone . . .'

"Then Satan took him to Jerusalem to the roof of the Temple." The great southeast corner of the temple area was the vivid setting for Jesus' next temptation. *" 'Jump off,' he said, 'and prove you are the Son of God . . .' "*
Matthew 4:5,6

Galilee fishing-boats

"One day as Jesus was walking along the shores of the Sea of Galilee, he saw Simon and his brother Andrew fishing with nets, for they were commercial fishermen. Jesus called out to them, 'Come, follow me! And I will make you fishermen for the souls of men!' At once they left their nets and went along with him. A little farther up the beach, he saw Zebedee's sons, James and John, in a boat mending their nets. He called them too. . . ." Mark 1:16-20

The Galilee fishing industry was a sizeable one in New Testament times. The fish was dried and taken to Jerusalem (via the 'Fish Gate'). John's detailed knowledge of Jerusalem suggests that the family business may have had a 'city office' there. A reference in Pliny to the fish pickled at Tarichaea by Galilee shows that it was exported throughout the Mediterranean world.

Cana in Galilee

"Two days later Jesus' mother was a guest at a wedding in the village of Cana in Galilee, and Jesus and his disciples were invited too."
John 2:1,2

The name 'Cana' is preserved in the present-day village of Kafr Kana, a few miles east of Nazareth in the Galilean hills. John selects the wedding where Jesus turned water into wine as the first of the 'signs' in his Gospel. The water was for 'the Jewish rites of purification': Jesus had come to bring the wine of the new age, the gospel.

Villagers still come to the well in Kafr Kana to draw water.

Capernaum

"Jesus and his companions now arrived at . . . Capernaum and on Saturday . . . went into . . . the synagogue—where he preached. The congregation was surprised at his sermon because he spoke as an authority. . . ." Mark 1:21,22

Capernaum was Jesus' base for much of his teaching and healing ministry in Galilee. It was the home town of Peter and Andrew. It was also the place where the Roman centurion whose slave was healed by Jesus had built a synagogue (Luke 7: 5). The ruin of the synagogue on the site of Capernaum dates from the second century, but it shows the same combination of Roman architecture with Jewish symbolism that would also have characterized the earlier one.

The palm, a symbol of the land of Israel, carved on the synagogue stone-work.

More Jewish symbols: a bunch of grapes and a star.

Galilee countryside

"He began a tour of the cities and villages of Galilee to announce the coming of the Kingdom of God, and took his twelve disciples with him." Luke 8:1

Behind the hills which flank the edge of the Plain of Jezreel lies Nazareth. The village in the foreground is at the foot of Mount Tabor. In New Testament times Galilee was at the intersection of important trade-routes: Jesus' teaching was in no backwater but in a busy, if second-class, province of the Roman Empire.

Known as the 'Mount of Precipitation' this rocky hill is just near Nazareth. It might well have been where Jesus was taken when the outraged inhabitants of Nazareth threatened to 'throw him down headlong'. The claims of Jesus were too much for the people of his own home town.

City on a hill

*"You are the world's light—
a city on a hill, glowing in the
night for all to see. Don't hide your
light! Let it shine for all; let your good
deeds glow for all to see, so that
they will praise your heavenly Father."*
Matthew 5:14-16

Much of the teaching of Jesus was in the
form of object-lessons and parables from
life around. The 'city on a hill' pictured
here is Tsefat in Upper Galilee, for long a
centre of Jewish learning and devotion.

Oil-lamps typical
of the very many
found from Roman
and later periods
(Archaeological
Museum, Istanbul)

*"Don't do your
good deeds
publicly, to be
admired"*
Matthew 6:1

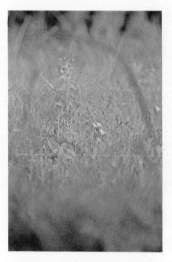

*"Why worry about
your clothes?
Look at the field
lilies!"*
Matthew 6:28

Jacob's Well

"Around noon as he approached the village of Sychar, he came to Jacob's Well, located on the parcel of ground Jacob gave to his son Joseph. Jesus was tired from the long walk in the hot sun and sat wearily beside the well. Soon a Samaritan woman came to draw water. . . ." John 4:5-7

This well is typical of those still in use in country areas. Not only racial prejudice (verse 9) but also the fact that women were despised (verse 27) made it surprising that Jesus stopped to talk to the woman of Samaria. But the result was a vital conversation: 'Whoever drinks of the water I shall give shall never thirst . . .'

Jacob's well itself is now enclosed within a church; it is still true that 'the well is deep'; and the water is as good as when Jacob first dug it.

The Good Shepherd

". . . The sheep hear his voice and come to him; and he calls his own sheep by name and leads them out. He walks ahead of them; and they follow him, for they recognize his voice. . . . 'I am the Good Shepherd.' " John 10:3,4,11

Traditionally the Eastern shepherd would not drive his sheep but lead them. When several flocks were mixed they could be separated simply by the shepherd's call to his own sheep. At night when they were in a sheepfold of rocks and stone walls the shepherd would lie across the door to protect them: he was also the 'door of the sheep'.

Nain

"Jesus went with his disciples to the village of Nain, with the usual great crowd at his heels. A funeral procession was coming out as he approached the village gate. The boy who had died was the only son of his widowed mother. . . . When the Lord saw her, his heart overflowed with sympathy. . . ." Luke 7:11-13

A village on the slope of a hill looking towards the rounded hump of Mt Tabor, Nain was the scene of the demonstration of the power of Jesus over death itself.

Storm over the lake

*"A terrible storm arose.
High waves began to break into
the boat until it was nearly full
of water and about to sink. . . . Then he
rebuked the wind and said to the sea,
'Quiet down!'"* Mark 4:37, 39

Jesus claimed power not only over sickness and death itself, but also over creation: 'Who then is this, that even wind and sea obey him?' (verse 41). Fishing boats used on the Lake of Galilee are small; and a storm can soon blot out the coast-line and raise a heavy sea.

Lake of Galilee

*"Jesus told his disciples to get
into their boat and cross to the other
side of the lake while he stayed to get
the people started home."* Matthew 14:22

Jesus used the lake as an escape-route from the crowds. He taught the people on the beach from a boat. The lake was used to teach his disciples faith. This view is of the north-western corner of it, looking from near Tiberias toward the site of Magdala and Gennesaret.

The Sower

"He used many illustrations such as this . . . 'A farmer was sowing grain in his fields. As he scattered the seed across the ground, some fell beside a path, and the birds came and ate it. And some fell on rocky soil . . . among thorns . . . on good soil. . . .' " Matthew 13:3-8

Jesus spoke in parables, using everyday examples to get his message across. But he also used parables to appeal to people's will as much as to their understanding: only people who really wanted to follow him would grasp the meaning, not the wilfully blind or those who had no intention of obeying (Matthew 13:10-17). The picture of the 'soils' was taken in Galilee; Mt Moreh is in the background.

The Good Samaritan

"A Jew going on a trip from Jerusalem to Jericho was attacked by bandits. They stripped him of his clothes and money and beat him up and left him lying half dead. . . ." Luke 10:30

Jesus' story of the man who was beaten up on the Jericho road would have been only too real to his hearers in Jerusalem. The road passes through rocky, desert country as it winds down to Jericho in the Jordan valley. The ruin of an inn still stands where an inn has stood for centuries. But the twist in the story may not have proved so easy to accept: it was a despised Samaritan, not the religious people, who showed true love for his neighbour.

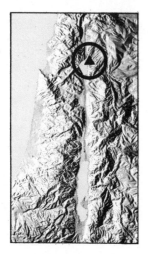

Lakeside miracles

"When they arrived at the other side of the lake a demon-possessed man ran out from a graveyard, just as Jesus was climbing from the boat. . . . And Jesus gave them permission. Then the evil spirits came out of the man and entered the hogs, and the entire herd plunged down the steep hillside into the lake. . . ."
Mark 5:1,2,13

The district of Gerasa, Gadara and Gergesa was east of the Lake of Galilee, an area known for its 'ten towns', or decapolis, occupied by Greeks: this would explain why there was so large a herd of swine, for pork was a forbidden food for the Jew. The picture looks toward the north-eastern end of the lake.

It was at the north-east end of the lake, too, that a crowd of five thousand were fed from five loaves and two small fishes. These fish are known today as 'St Peter's Fish' because of their large mouth (in which they carry their eggs); see Matthew 17:27. The fish in the story of the feeding of the five thousand may well, however, have been pickled, or salted, rather than fresh.

44

Caesarea Philippi

*"When Jesus came to Caesarea Philippi,
he asked his disciples, 'Who are the
people saying I am?' . . . Simon Peter
answered, 'The Christ, the Messiah, the
Son of the living God.' Jesus said, . . .
'You are Peter, a stone; and upon this
rock I will build my church. . . .'"*
Matthew 16:13,16-18

Caesarea Philippi was built by the
tetrarch Philip (son of Herod the Great)
and dedicated to 'Caesar', the Roman
Emperor. It was formerly known as
Paneas, derived from the veneration of
the Great God Pan. So it was against
the background both of Emperor-worship
and 'pantheism' that Peter made his
confession; and against the background
of a rock cliff which dominates one of
the sources of the Jordan.

Mount Hermon

"Jesus took Peter, James, and his brother John to the top of a high and lonely hill, and as they watched, his appearance changed so that his face shone like the sun and his clothing became dazzling white . . . and a voice from the cloud said, 'This is my beloved Son, and I am wonderfully pleased with him. Obey him.' " Matthew 17:1,2,5

Mount Hermon is very near Caesarea Philippi, and so it has long been supposed that this mountain was the site of the transfiguration. It is certainly a 'high mountain', rising to 9,100 ft, and dominating Upper Galilee. The picture is of dawn over Mt Hermon.

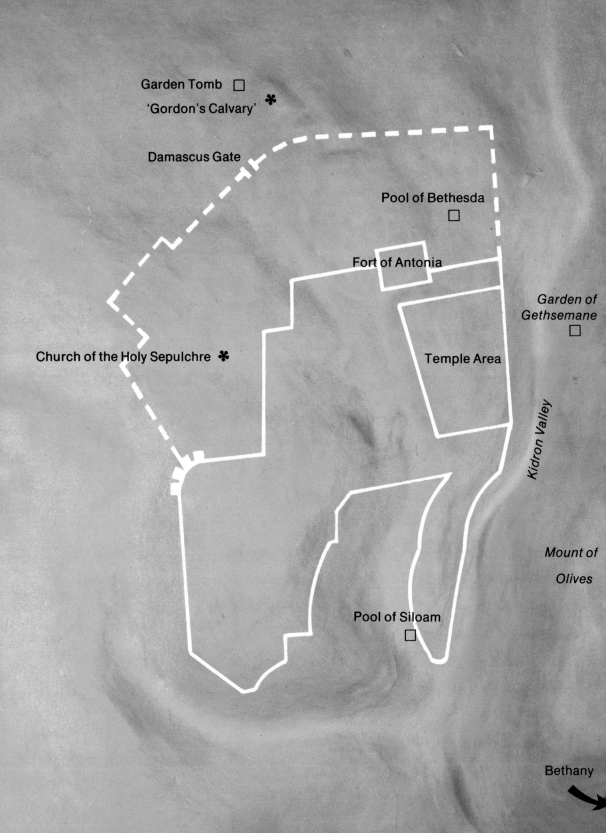

Garden Tomb ☐
'Gordon's Calvary' ✳

Damascus Gate

Pool of Bethesda ☐

Fort of Antonia

Garden of
Gethsemane ☐

Church of the Holy Sepulchre ✳

Temple Area

Kidron Valley

Mount of
Olives

Pool of Siloam ☐

Bethany

PART TWO

Opposition and Triumph

Synagogue

"Jesus went . . . to the synagogue . . . and noticed a man . . . with a deformed hand. Since it was the Sabbath, Jesus' enemies watched. . . . Would he heal the man's hand? If he did, they planned to arrest him!"

Mark 3:1,2

From the beginning of his ministry Jesus taught in the Jewish synagogues. But the religious leaders who had reduced the law to a tyranny of petty rules strongly resented every move he made to restore the true meaning of God's law.

Another synagogue: both are in Tsefat, in Galilee.

An orthodox Jew with a phylactery— passages from the law in a small box— bound to his forehead in literal obedience to commandments such as Deuteronomy 6:8.

The clash with orthodoxy

"Some Pharisees and other Jewish leaders now arrived from Jerusalem to interview Jesus. 'Why do your disciples disobey the ancient Jewish traditions?' they demanded. 'For they ignore our ritual of ceremonial handwashing before they eat.' He replied, 'And why do your traditions violate the direct commandments of God?' "
Matthew 15:1-3

In such places as Tsefat, pictured here, and the Mea Shearim quarter of Jerusalem today, ultra-orthodox Jews seek to live out the minutiae of the observance of the law and rabbinic traditions.

Those who led 'little ones' astray were fit only to have a mill-stone tied round their necks and be cast into the sea.

Jesus compared the Pharisees to 'whited sepulchres', tombs whitewashed outside but rotten inside.

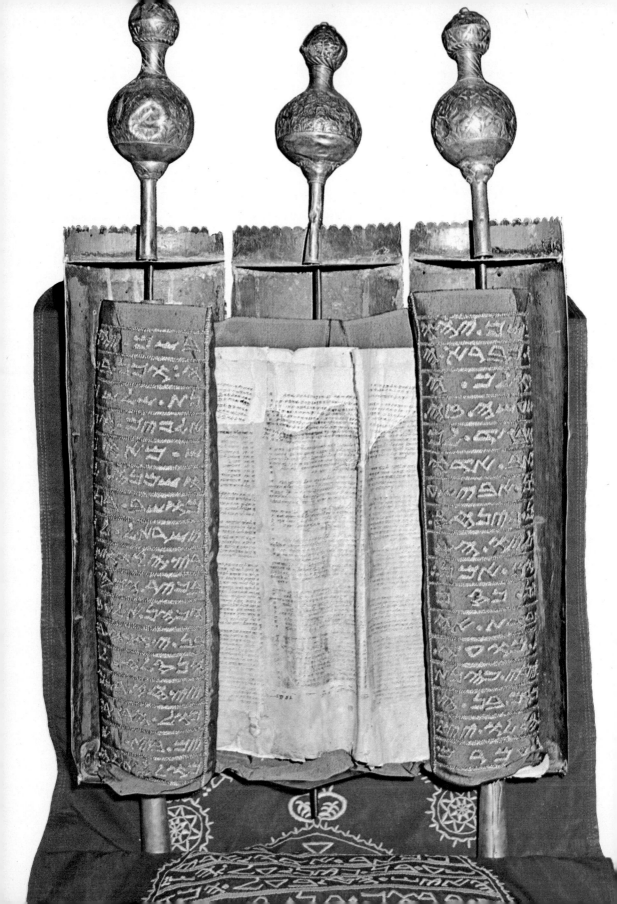

The law

*"Don't misunderstand why I have come—
it isn't to cancel the laws of Moses and the
warnings of the prophets. No, I came
to fulfill them. . . . With all the earnestness
I have I say: Every law in the Book
will continue until its purpose is
achieved."* Matthew 5:17,18

This ancient scroll of the Pentateuch,
the first five books of the Bible, belongs
to the Samaritan synagogue in Nablus,
near ancient Shechem.

An orthodox Jew studying the law.

Jerusalem

*"O Jerusalem, Jerusalem! The city that
murders the prophets. . . . stones those sent
to help her. . . . I have wanted to gather
your children together even as a hen pro-
tects her brood under her wings, but you
wouldn't let me."* Luke 13:34

The Old City of Jerusalem is enclosed by
walls dating back to medieval times. It
is a square-shaped maze of narrow
streets and ancient buildings. The more
modern buildings of the new Jerusalem
rise behind. The gate is known as St
Stephen's Gate after the first Christian
martyr—whose death was a grim
confirmation of Jesus' lament over the
city.

57

The Pool of Bethesda

"Inside the city, near the Sheep Gate, was Bethesda Pool, with five covered platforms or porches surrounding it. Crowds of sick folks . . . lay on the platforms. . . . One . . . lying there had been sick for thirty-eight years. . . . Jesus told him, 'Stand up, roll up your sleeping mat and go on home!' " John 5:2-5,8

Archaeologists discovered, deep below the present level of Jerusalem, a pool with five porticoes . . . Mixed with remains from Crusader times there is stonework going back to the time of Jesus himself, and earlier.

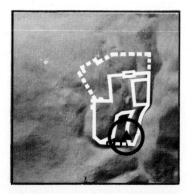

The Pool of Siloam is associated with another miracle of Jesus in Jerusalem: the healing of the man blind from birth (John 9). It goes back to the engineering feat of Hezekiah about 700 BC, when a rock tunnel 1,700 ft long was dug to bring water inside the city from a spring outside.

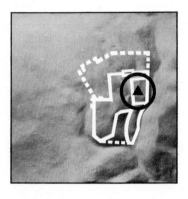

The Temple Area

"Every day Jesus went to the Temple to teach, and the crowds began gathering early in the morning to hear him. And each evening he returned to spend the night on the Mount of Olives."
Luke 21:37,38

The large temple area, formerly resplendent with courts and porticoes, is now almost bare except for two large mosques. The golden-domed Mosque of Omar stands over the rock of Mount Moriah, where Abraham showed his willingness to sacrifice his son Isaac. It was in the courtyards of the temple that the money-changers and sellers of 'official' sacrifices were fleecing the poor. Teachers would gather their disciples around them in the Temple porticoes. Here too the early church met. 'They were all together in Solomon's Portico' (Acts 5:12).

Inscription in Greek forbidding Gentiles on pain of death to enter the temple precincts (see Acts 21:28) (Istanbul Archaeological Museum).

Teaching on the end

"But when you see Jerusalem surrounded by armies, then you will know that the time of its destruction has arrived. Then let the people of Judea flee to the hills." Luke 21:20,21

In the course of his teaching on the final events up to the end of time Jesus dramatically foretold the destruction of Jerusalem—which happened some forty years later in AD 70. In a relief on the Titus Arch in Rome, plunder from the Temple of Jerusalem is seen being carried in triumph by the victorious Romans.

In 1947 the Dead Sea Scrolls, manuscripts of Old Testament books, were discovered in a cave, untouched since they had been hidden there before the Roman army over-ran the area in AD 68. Nearby are the remains of Qumran, the settlement of a monastic Jewish community which owned the manuscripts: there are clear evidences of violent destruction in the ruins.

Jerusalem street

"Some of the people . . . in Jerusalem said among themselves, 'Isn't this the man they are trying to kill? But here he is preaching in public, and they say nothing to him. Can it be that our leaders have learned . . . that he really is the Messiah? . . . After all . . . what miracles do you expect the Messiah to do that this man hasn't done?' When the Pharisees heard . . . this . . . they and the chief priests sent officers to arrest Jesus."
John 7:25,26,31,32

In the tangle of crowded narrow streets in the old city of Jerusalem it is easy to imagine the rumor and intrigue which surrounded the last days of the ministry of Jesus. The conflict with the religious leaders was coming to a head. The city was full of pilgrims, in Jerusalem for the Festival of the Passover. Tension was at breaking-point.

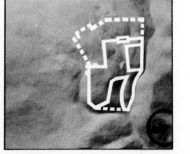

The nearby village of Bethany offered Jesus a refuge away from the crowded city. It was the home of Martha, Mary and Lazarus—and the scene of one of Jesus' most striking miracles (John 11).

The vine

*"I am the Vine; you are the branches.
Whoever lives in me and I in him shall
produce . . . fruit. For apart from me you
can't do a thing. If anyone separates
from me, he is thrown away like a useless
branch. . . ."* John 15:5,6

It was after the Last Supper, in the course
of the Passover Feast, that Jesus taught
his close disciples about their coming
relationship to himself. Each branch of
a vine grows directly from the main
'stock'. After the grapes are picked the
branches are cut right back, nearly to the
stock. For much of the year the stock
grows round them—they 'abide' in the
vine. Then the new branches grow out
rapidly to bear fruit. Branches which do
not bear fruit are cut off altogether:
they are of no use for anything but to
be burnt.

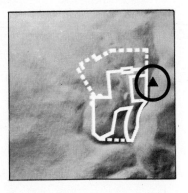

Gethsemane

"After saying these things Jesus crossed the Kidron ravine with his disciples and entered a grove of olive trees." John 18:1

Down from the walls of the old city, across a small valley, and up the slopes of the Mt of Olives opposite, there was a secluded garden where, John tells us, Jesus often met with his disciples. In the Garden of Gethsemane the tortured forms of these ancient olive trees, centuries old, still recall the agony which Jesus went through before his final arrest, as he faced the horror of a death in which he would be bearing the evil and alienation of human sin and separation from his Father.

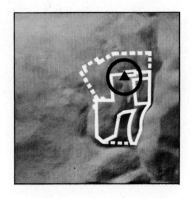

The Pavement

*"Next he was taken to the palace
of the Roman governor. . . . Then Pilate
tried to release him, but the Jewish
leaders told him, 'If you release this man,
you are no friend of Caesar's. Anyone
who declares himself a king is a
rebel against Caesar.' At these words
Pilate brought Jesus out to them again
and sat down at the judgment bench
on the stone-paved platform. . . . Pilate
said to the Jews, 'Here is your king!'
'Away with him,' they yelled.
'Away with him—crucify him!' "*
John 18:28; 19:12-15

The actual 'Pavement' of the Roman Fort
of Antonia (the praetorium) was recently
discovered under the Sisters of Zion
Convent in Jerusalem. Scratched on some
of the paving stones are the games the
Roman soldiers once played. (This one
is said to be for the ancient 'game of a
king'. Traditionally the loser lost his life
—it was a game often played with con-
demned prisoners. Kings would play it
themselves—and if they lost have a
slave put to death on their behalf.)

Place of a Skull

"And they brought Jesus to a place called Golgotha. (Golgotha means skull.) Wine drugged with bitter herbs was offered to him there, but he refused it. And then they crucified him—and threw dice for his clothes. It was about nine o'clock in the morning when the crucifixion took place."
Mark 15:22-25

It is not certain precisely where Jesus was crucified. Traditionally it is on the site now marked by the Church of the Holy Sepulchre, which was formerly outside the city walls. Research on the location of the walls in New Testament times continues. It was General Gordon in the last century who suggested that this rocky outcrop outside the present northern wall bore a striking resemblance to the shape of a skull.

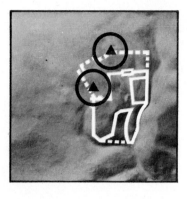

The empty tomb

"The next evening, when the Sabbath ended, Mary Magdalene and Salome and Mary the mother of James went out and purchased embalming spices. Early the following morning, just at sunrise, they carried them out to the tomb. On the way they were discussing how they could ever roll aside the huge stone from the entrance. But when they arrived they looked up and saw that the stone— a very heavy one—was already moved away. . . ." Mark 16:1-4

In an ancient garden just near 'Gordon's Calvary' outside the walls of Jerusalem is this tomb, a vivid example of the type in which Jesus was laid. A groove in front took the great stone which was rolled in front of the entrance.

Looking out from inside another first-century tomb, the stone in place by the entrance. This one was recently discovered in Nazareth beneath the Convent of the Sisters of Nazareth.

Inside, the body was 'bound in linen cloths with the spices' (John 19:40) and laid on a stone slab. When Peter came to the tomb of Jesus, 'he saw the linen cloths lying, and the napkin, which had been on his head, not lying with the linen cloths but rolled up in a place by itself. . . ' (John 20:6, 7). The body had gone, but the cloths had been left intact.

The great commission

"The eleven disciples left for Galilee, going to the mountain where Jesus had said they would find him. There they . . . worshiped him—but some . . . weren't sure it really was Jesus! He told his disciples, 'I have been given all authority in heaven and earth. Therefore go and make disciples in all the nations. . . .' "
Matthew 28:16-19

Looking towards the peaks of Mt Hermon in Upper Galilee.

Some of Jesus' resurrection appearances were in Jerusalem, some in Galilee. One took place on the shore of the Lake of Galilee, where the disciples had returned to their fishing. Jesus had prepared a fire on the beach and shared a breakfast of fish and bread with his disciples. Afterwards he gave to Peter, who had denied him three times, the opportunity to re-affirm three times his love for his Master. 'Jesus said to him, "Feed my sheep" ' (John 21).

79

Ascension

" 'When the Holy Spirit has come
upon you, you will receive power to
testify about me . . . to the people . . .
throughout the earth.' . . . It was not long
afterwards that he rose into the sky and
disappeared into a cloud, leaving
them staring after him."
Acts 1:8,9

Luke also tells us where the ascension
took place—on the Mount of Olives, the
hill overlooking Jerusalem across the
Kidron valley. (The tower is of a church
commemorating the event.) And with
the ascension came the promise that
Jesus would come again.

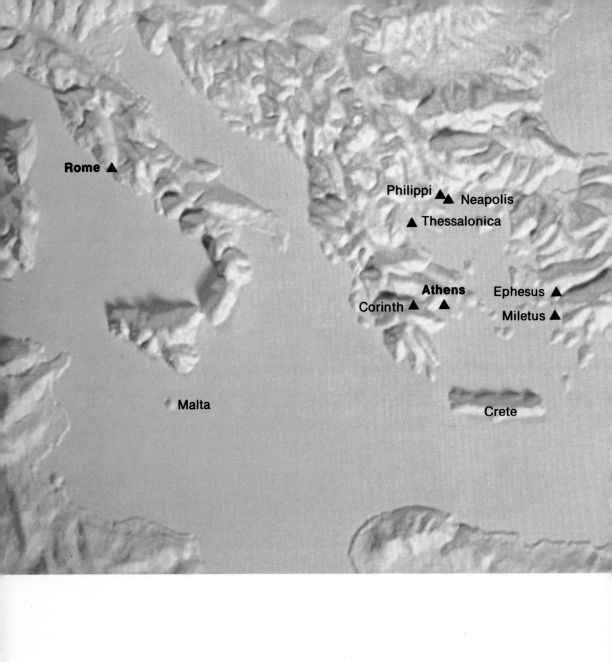

Rome ▲

Philippi ▲▲ Neapolis

▲ Thessalonica

Athens

Corinth ▲ ▲

Ephesus ▲

Miletus ▲

Malta

Crete

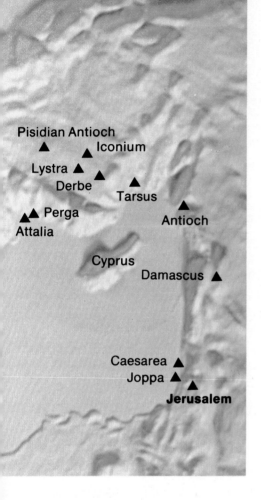

Pisidian Antioch ▲
▲ ▲ Iconium
Lystra ▲
▲ Derbe
Tarsus ▲
▲▲ Perga
Attalia
▲ Antioch

Cyprus
Damascus ▲

Caesarea ▲
Joppa ▲
▲ **Jerusalem**

PART THREE

Outreach of the Early Church

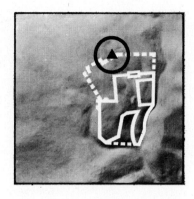

Pentecost

*"Pentecost had now arrived.
As the believers met together that
day. . . . everyone present was filled with
the Holy Spirit and began speaking in
languages they didn't know, . . . godly Jews
. . . in Jerusalem that day for the religious
celebrations, having arrived from
many nations. . . . were stunned to hear
their own languages being spoken
by the disciples."*
Acts 2:1,4-6

The medieval Damascus Gate in Jerusalem was the starting-point of the trade-
route to Damascus in Syria. In New
Testament times, too, Jerusalem was a
cosmopolitan city with trade and religious
links throughout the ancient world.
The Feast of Pentecost brought
together Jews from far and wide (see
verses 9-11). The immediate result of
the giving of the Holy Spirit was
Peter's powerful address to this inter-
national gathering.

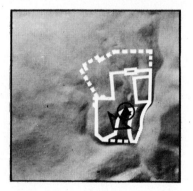

Persecution and outreach

*". . . And dragged him out of the city to
stone him. . . . A great wave of persecution of the believers began that day,
sweeping over the church in Jerusalem,
and everyone except the apostles fled
into Judea and Samaria. (But some godly
Jews came and with great sorrow buried
Stephen.)"* Acts 7:58; 8:1,2

The communal life and fellowship of the
church in Jerusalem was not left in peace
for long. Stephen was the first martyr of
the new faith. His death triggered off fresh
persecution. But the immediate effect of
this was to spread the gospel more
widely. There was also another, longer
term effect: the impact of Stephen's
death on the mind of a young man
named Saul.

Samaria

"When the apostles back in Jerusalem heard that the people of Samaria had accepted God's message, they sent down Peter and John. . . . After testifying and preaching in Samaria, Peter and John returned to Jerusalem, stopping at several Samaritan villages . . . to preach . . . to them too." Acts 8:14,25

The hill-country of Samaria, north from Jerusalem, and Judea, south from Jerusalem, were the first obvious starting-points for the outreach of the gospel. The village pictured here is near the ancient capital of Samaria. Orthodox Jews steered clear of the area for they despised the Samaritans: they were of mixed race, and held rival sacrifices. The early Christians, particularly Philip, 'proclaimed to them the Christ'.

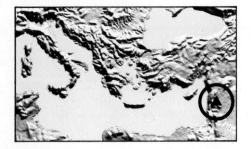

The road to Damascus

"Paul . . . eager to destroy every Christian, went to the High Priest. . . . He requested a letter . . . to synagogues in Damascus, requiring their cooperation in the persecution of any believers he found there, . . . so that he could bring them in chains to Jerusalem. As he was nearing Damascus . . . suddenly a brilliant light from heaven spotted down upon him!"
Acts 9:1-3

Saul, who became the apostle Paul, was later to describe several times the dramatic events on the Damascus road. The risen Christ himself spoke unmistakably to him. In persecuting the church he had been persecuting Jesus himself. Saul fell to the ground. And when he rose he was blind, and had to be led by the hand into Damascus.

Paul was born in Tarsus, a large Romanized city and university town in what is now south-east Turkey. Pompey and Cicero were two famous Romans who had been involved in its government, and it was visited by Antony. Little remains from Roman times except this arch. But the fact that Paul was a Roman citizen was to be decisive in later events.

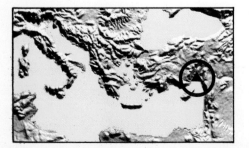

90

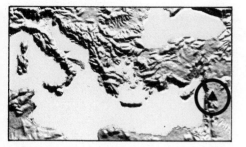

The Street called Straight

"Now there was in Damascus a believer named Ananias. The Lord spoke to him in a vision. . . . And the Lord said, 'Go over to Straight Street and find the house of a man named Judas and ask there for Paul of Tarsus. He is praying. . . .'"
Acts 9:10,11

The Street called Straight in Damascus is today a busy artery of the old covered markets. A Roman gateway at one end and ancient walls show what was once the extent of the city. Paul 'was without sight, and neither ate nor drank' for three days. His identification with his Lord's own death and resurrection to newness of life was then sealed as Ananias baptized him. It was in Damascus that he first preached, in the numerous synagogues; and on his return there later he had to escape by being lowered ignominiously down from a window in the city wall.

Joppa

" 'Cornelius! . . . Send some men to Joppa to find a man named Simon Peter, who is staying with Simon, the tanner, down by the shore, and ask him to come and visit you.' . . . Peter went up on the flat roof of his house to pray. It was noon and he was hungry, but while lunch was being prepared, he fell into a trance."
Acts 10:3,5,6,9,10

This flat roof in Jaffa has lattice-work as a shade against the sun. The equivalent at the house of Simon the tanner would have been an awning tied at the corners. In his trance Peter saw 'a great sheet' filled with creatures both 'clean' and 'unclean' by Jewish law. 'What God has cleansed', he was told, 'you must not call common.' The implications became clear when he visited Cornelius. The gospel was not only for Jews, but also for the Gentiles.

Antioch

"Barnabas went on to Tarsus to hunt for Paul. When he found him, he brought him back to Antioch; and both of them stayed there for a full year, teaching the many new converts. (It was there at Antioch that the believers were first called 'Christians.')" Acts 11:25, 26

Antioch, on the River Orontes, was capital of the Roman province of Syria and the third largest city of the Empire. So it was perhaps natural that its Christian church should have been fast-growing and energetic. It sent money for famine relief to the church in Jerusalem. At Antioch 'overseas missions' were born when the church sent out Paul and Barnabas. The church challenged those in Jerusalem who insisted on Jewish traditions. The town is today called Antakya, in the south-eastern corner of Turkey near the border with Syria.

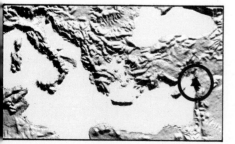

Cyprus

"One day as these men were worshiping and fasting the Holy Spirit said, 'Dedicate Barnabas and Paul for a special job I have for them.' Directed by the Holy Spirit they went to Seleucia and then sailed for Cyprus. There, in the town of Salamis, they went to the Jewish synagogue and preached."
Acts 13:2,4,5

Salamis was the first stop in this first missionary journey. Paul and Barnabas set the pattern for their work by preaching first in the Jewish synagogues. Salamis today consists of extensive ruins scattered over an area of sand-dune and woodland near Famagusta. The theatre, gymnasium (pictured here), harbour and other remains evoke something of the prosperous city which confronted the missionaries with all the power of a predominantly Roman culture.

aphos, at the other end of Cyprus, was where Paul met the proconsul Sergius Paulus. The Roman ruins pictured here may have been the proconsul's residence; or remains of the forum.

Today extensive Roman, Hellenistic and Byzantine ruins surround the harbour from which Paul and Barnabas sailed for the next stage of their mission.

Pisidian Antioch

"Now Paul and those with him left Paphos by ship for Turkey, landing at the port town of Perga. There John deserted them and returned to Jerusalem. But Barnabas and Paul went on to Antioch, a city in the province of Pisidia. On the Sabbath they went into the synagogue for the services. . . . Paul stood, waved a greeting to them and began. 'Men of Israel,' he said, 'and all others here who reverence God. . . .'" Acts 13:13,14,16

In making first for Perga (see page 105) and then Pisidian Antioch Paul pursued the same policy which later took him to Athens and Rome. He deliberately made for main centers from which the gospel would be taken to the surrounding district by the converts rather than the missionaries. Pisidian Antioch was a center of Hellenistic Greek and Roman culture with a considerable Jewish settlement. High in what is now central Turkey, it had a magnificent setting. The Roman aqueducts pictured here once brought water to the city which now lies in ruins.

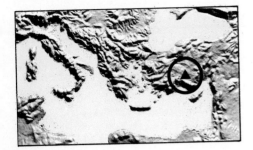

Lystra

"When the . . . crowd saw what Paul had done, they shouted . . . 'These men are gods in human bodies!' They decided that Barnabas was the Greek god Jupiter, and that Paul, because he was the chief speaker, was Mercury! The local priest of the Temple of Jupiter, located on the outskirts of the city, brought them cartloads of flowers and prepared to sacrifice oxen to them at the city gates before the crowds." Acts 14:11-13

The setting of Lystra is a landscape of rocks, mountains and fertile plain. Faced, not now with Jews, but with superstitious pagans, the missionaries had to change their tactics. They started from God as Creator, 'the living God who made the heaven and the earth . . .' Today the nearby site of Lystra itself is no more than a litter of fallen stones.

Head of Hermes, found at Pergamum (Izmir Archaeological Museum)

Attalia

"They . . . preached again in Perga, and went on to Attalia. Finally they returned by ship to Antioch, where their journey had begun, and where they had been committed to God for the work now completed." Acts 14:24-26

A trading schooner lies in the small harbour of the modern resort town of Antalya, formerly Attalia, on the south coast of Turkey.

Extensive ruins remain at Perga, a short distance inland, which the missionaries visited on both their outward and return journeys.

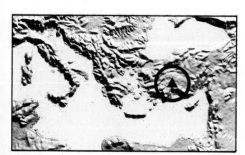

Pisidia

"Several days later Paul suggested to Barnabas that they return again to Turkey, and visit each city where they had preached before, to see how the new converts were getting along." Acts 15:36

The second missionary journey retraced the steps of the first before breaking new ground. Their route took them hundreds of miles across the mountains and plains of what is now central Turkey.

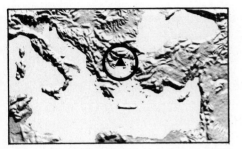

Neapolis

"That night Paul had a vision. In his dream he saw a man over in Macedonia, Greece, pleading with him, 'Come over here and help us.' . . . We went aboard a boat at Troas, and sailed straight across to Samothrace, and the next day on to Neapolis. . . ."
Acts 16:9,11

As the missionaries stepped ashore at Neapolis, modern Kavalla in northern Greece, they brought the gospel for the first time to Europe. Luke's account changes suddenly at Troas from 'they' to 'we'. Was he the man from Macedonia whose urgent requests for help gave Paul his night-time vision of the need 'to go on into Macedonia'?

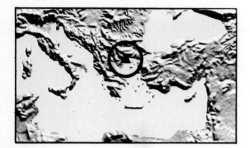

Philippi

". . . And finally reached Philippi, a Roman colony just inside the Macedonian border, and stayed there several days. . . ."
Acts 16:12

It was characteristic of Paul's tactics that he made for the leading city of the district. It may also have been Luke's own hometown. The official names translated as 'rulers' (verse 19), 'magistrates' (verse 20), 'police' (verse 35) are precise and reflect Philippi's civic pride in its status as a Roman colony. The picture is of the Forum, with the ruins of a Byzantine basilica behind. Several places nearby could have been the 'riverside' where there was a 'place of prayer' (some of the streams are now being drained in the interests of mosquito control and irrigation).

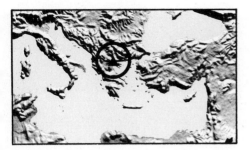

The road to Thessalonica

"Now they traveled through the cities of Amphipolis and Apollonia and came to Thessalonica, where there was a Jewish synagogue. As was Paul's custom, he went there to preach, and for three Sabbaths in a row he opened the Scriptures to the people. . . ." Acts 17:1,2

The Via Egnatia was the main east-west Roman road, linking the west coast of Greece with what is now Istanbul. The stone slabs worn into ruts by the wheels of the traffic were those on which Paul and his companions trod as they made for Thessalonica, then as now the most prominent city of the region.

Today Thessaloniki is the second largest city in Greece. In later Roman times the Via Egnatia passed under the Arch of Galerius pictured here. The street is still called by the same name.

Athens

"While Paul was waiting for them in Athens, he was deeply troubled by all the idols he saw everywhere throughout the city. He went to the synagogue for discussions with the Jews and the devout Gentiles, and spoke daily in the public square to all who happened to be there. But they invited him to the forum at Mars Hill. 'Come and tell us more about this new religion,' they said."
Acts 17:16,17,19

Behind the agora, or market-place, at Athens rises the Acropolis (to the left), and Mars Hill, or the Areopagus (to the right). It was this hill which gave its name to the Council of the Areopagus which formerly met there. In Paul's day it met in one of the colonnaded buildings flanking the agora itself. It was before this learned body that Paul was taken to submit his 'new teaching'.

The Acropolis of Athens was a fortified sanctuary which was both the center of its worship and its ultimate defensive position against invaders. The Parthenon, with which it is crowned, was built in the fifth century BC, the 'golden age' of Athens under Pericles. It has been successively a temple to the goddess Athena, a church, a mosque, a gunpowder store—and a shrine of classicism and tourism.

Corinth

"The leader of the synagogue, and all his household believed . . . and were baptized . . . . So Paul stayed there the next year and a half, teaching the truths of God. But when Gallio became governor of Achaia, the Jews rose . . . against Paul and brought him before the governor. . . ."
Acts 18:8,11,12

The Temple of Apollo dominates the ancient site of Corinth today. Behind rises the fortress of Acro-Corinth. Near the temple the agora, or market-place, contains the remains of shops, temples, fountains, houses — and the 'bema', the official rostrum from which the Roman governor spoke. See too the picture on page 136.

Ephesus: the temple

"Paul has persuaded many, many people that handmade gods aren't gods at all. As a result, . . . sales volume is going down! . . . throughout the entire province! Of course, I am not only talking about . . . loss of income, but also of the possibility that the temple of . . . Diana will lose its influence, and that Diana—this magnificent goddess worshiped not only throughout this part of Turkey but all around the world—will be forgotten!" Acts 19:26,27

Demetrius and his fellow silversmiths found that the effects of the Christian gospel were threatening their trade in 'silver shrines of Artemis'. The great Temple of Artemis, or Diana, was one of the wonders of the ancient world. It is now a great rectangular area of marsh and water littered with broken pillars.

The nearby Museum of Ephesus contains two larger-than-life-size statues of the goddess. This one is a Roman version in white marble. Diana was the Roman goddess of chastity, Artemis the Greek goddess of love. It is typical of the place that the two were identified—and merged with the ancient local fertility cults.

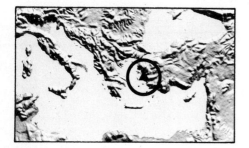

Ephesus: the theatre

"At this their anger boiled and they began shouting, 'Great is Diana of the Ephesians!' . . . The city was filled with confusion. Everyone rushed to the amphitheater. . . . Inside, the people were all shouting, some one thing and some another —everything was in confusion. . . . Most of them didn't even know why they were there." Acts 19:28,29,32

The theatre is but one of the magnificent and extensive remains still being uncovered by archaeologists at Ephesus. The road leads down to what was once the harbour, long since silted up.

The main street at Ephesus. Hadrian's Temple (see page 140) is on the left.

Miletus

*"At Miletus, he sent . . . to the elders
of the church at Ephesus asking them to
come down to the boat to meet him. When
they arrived he told them, 'You men know
that from the day I set foot in Turkey until
now I have done the Lord's work humbly . . .
with tears—and have faced grave danger
. . . . Now I am going to Jerusalem, drawn
there irresistibly by the Holy Spirit,
not knowing what awaits me.' "*
Acts 20:17-19,22

Miletus, 50 miles by road from Ephesus,
was another of the great cosmopolitan
cities of the west coast of Asia Minor,
colonies of Hellenistic Greek culture. Like
Ephesus, it boasts the remains of a
magnificent theatre. Seat reservations are
inscribed on the stone seats, including
one for Jews and God-fearers.

Paul reminded the Ephesian elders at
Miletus to look after their flock as
shepherds protect their sheep from
marauding wolves.

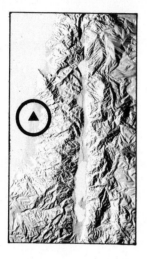

Caesarea

"So that night, as ordered, the soldiers took Paul to Antipatris. They returned to the armory the next morning, leaving him with the cavalry to take him on to Caesarea. When they arrived in Caesarea, they presented Paul and the letter to the governor."
Acts 23:31-33

Paul had already passed through Caesarea on his way to Jerusalem. He was brought back there ignominiously, under arrest and hurriedly removed from Jerusalem to save him from a Jewish plot. Caesarea was the center of local Roman government—and Paul was a Roman citizen. The governor Felix heard his case; then left him in prison for two years. His successor, Festus, and the puppet king Herod Agrippa then listened to his defence. But Paul appealed to Caesar. Roman pillars are washed by the sea in what remains of Caesarea; they were used to strengthen Crusader walls.

Statues, a theatre, a horse-racing stadium, aqueduct, and remains of harbour breakwaters remain from Roman times. An inscription bearing the name of Pilate was unearthed in 1961.

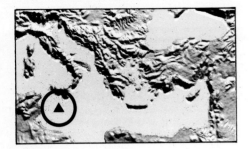

Malta

"When it was day, they didn't recognize the coastline, but noticed a bay with a beach and wondered whether they could get between the rocks and be driven up onto the beach. . . . But the ship hit a sandbar and ran aground. The bow . . . stuck fast . . . the stern . . . began to break apart. We soon learned that we were on the island of Malta."
Acts 27:39-41; 28:1

Storm and shipwreck meant a three-month delay in the journey to Rome. St Paul's Bay, as it is called today, meets the conditions of the description in Acts precisely. A shallow sandbank runs out from the distant spit of land: it was this the ship struck while they were making for the beach beyond. Their misfortune was the island's fortune: many, including the governor's father, found healing through Paul's prayers.

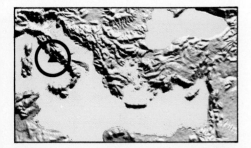

The road to Rome

"Then we went on to Rome. The brothers in Rome . . . came to meet us at the Forum on the Appian Way. Others joined us at The Three Taverns. When Paul saw them, he thanked God and took courage." Acts 28:14,15

Outside Rome the ancient Roman road the Via Appia is lined with monuments. Stretches of original paving, rutted by cart-wheels, are still used by modern traffic.

Rome

"Paul lived for the next two years in his rented house and welcomed all who visited him, telling them with all boldness about the Kingdom of God and about the Lord Jesus Christ; and no one tried to stop him." Acts 28:30,31

Paul had reached the heart of the ancient world. Whether or not he was able to fulfil his ambition to take the gospel to Spain, or whether he lived in Rome until the end of his days, we do not know. The Colosseum, the enormous amphitheatre built in AD 80, took its name from the colossal statue of Nero that stood near it. Here 45,000 spectators could watch fights between gladiators, even simulated naval battles. Here, when persecution later reached its height, Christians were thrown to lions to make sport for the crowds.

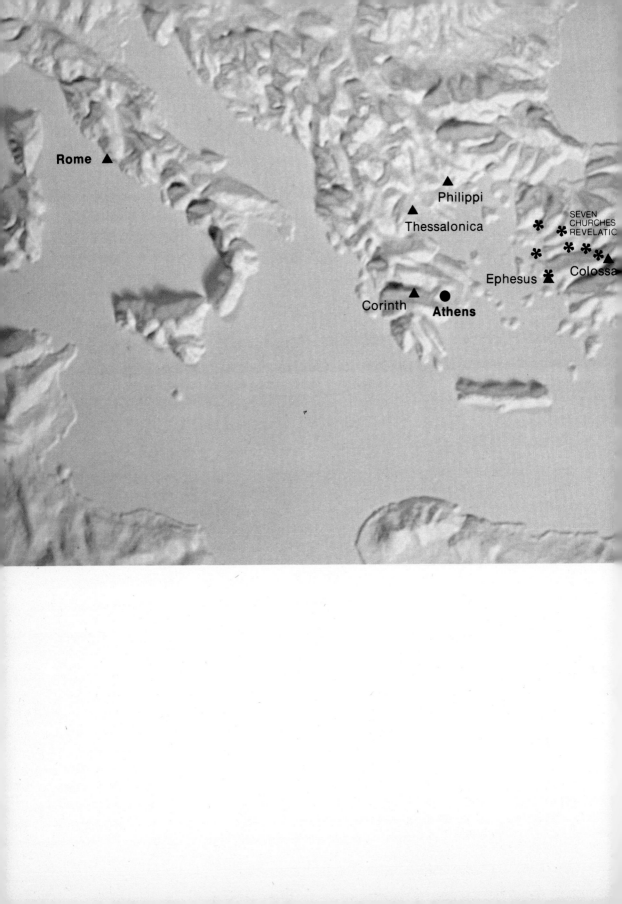

Rome ▲

▲
Philippi

▲
Thessalonica

SEVEN
CHURCHES
REVELATIC

✳   ✳

✳   ✳ ✳

Ephesus ✳   ▲
Colossa

▲
Corinth   ●
Athens

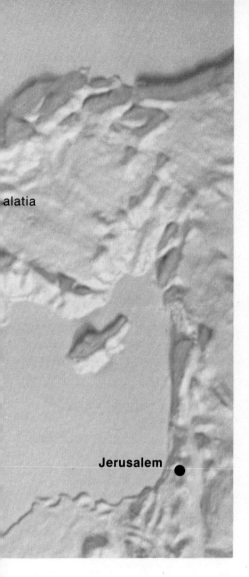

alatia

Jerusalem ●

PART FOUR

Letters to the Churches

Romans

"Tell Priscilla and Aquila 'hello.'. . . Greetings to all those who meet to worship in their home. Greet my good friend Epaenetus." Romans 16:3,5

Paul has a considerable list of greetings at the end of his letter to the Christians at Rome. There were in the church people of rank, members of the imperial household, people from Greek and Roman and Jewish backgrounds. The Forum at Rome was the city center with its main public buildings, and its principal meeting-place.

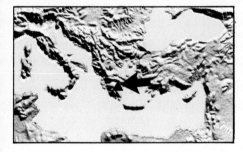

Corinthians

"Our bodies have many parts, but the many parts make up only one body. . . . So it is with the 'body' of Christ. Each of us is a part of the one body of Christ. Some of us are Jews, some are Gentiles, some are slaves and some are free." 1 Corinthians 12:12,13

Corinth was an industrial and trading city with a proverbial reputation for immorality. It had road-links with harbors on both sides of the narrow isthmus: the Lechaion road in this picture led to the principal port. Many of the Corinthian church's problems arose from its particular situation: the party divisions reflected the town's mixed population; there was open immorality; meat sold in the market came from pagan sacrifices; women must be veiled to avoid suspicion of prostitution; there were extremes of emphasis on Greek philosophy, or on spiritual gifts associated with the mystery religions. (See also page 116.)

Galatians

"Foolish Galatians! What magician has . . . cast an evil spell upon you? For you used to see the meaning of Jesus Christ's death . . . clearly. . . . Did you receive the Holy Spirit by trying to keep the Jewish laws?"
Galatians 3:1,2

It is a matter of debate whether Paul wrote to the Roman province of Galatia generally or the 'Galatian' or 'Gallic' people (settlers in the 3rd century BC) in the more northern part alone. But the purpose of the letter is clear: to prevent the churches giving in to Jewish elements who were denying the gospel by preaching 'salvation by law-keeping'. The picture is of a Jewish synagogue dating from the early centuries AD found at Sardis (one of the 'seven churches' of Revelation).

Ephesians

"What a foundation you stand on now: the apostles and the prophets; and the cornerstone of the building is Jesus Christ himself! We who believe are . . . joined together with Christ as parts of a . . . temple for God . . . joined with him and with each other by the Spirit . . ."
Ephesians 2:20-22

This Temple at Ephesus was dedicated to Hadrian, the Roman Emperor some years later than the time when this letter was written. It shows something of the splendor of the buildings of the time (see too page 120), and also illustrates the Emperor-worship which was to become a cause of persecution of the Christians for whom Jesus alone is Lord. At Smyrna, nearby, the aged Polycarp was to say before his martyrdom in AD 155, 'Eighty-six years have I served him, and he has done me no wrong; how then can I blaspheme my king who saved me?'

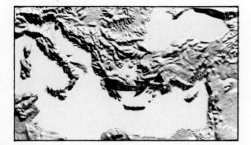

Colossians

"Christ is the exact likeness of the unseen God . . . and, in fact, Christ . . . is the Creator who made everything."
Colossians 1:15,16

Colossae was across a broad fertile valley from Laodicea and Hierapolis (see page 151). The mound of the ancient town, lying near the village of Honaz in the background of the picture, is yet to be excavated. Paul's letter was written to combat 'gnosticism'. Its combination of nature mysticism and speculations on created and uncreated beings would have appealed to a predominantly agricultural community in an area surrounded by mountains. As long ago as Heraclitus in the sixth century BC the people had been convinced that 'the world is full of spiritual beings'.

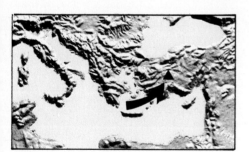

The Letters of Peter

"You have a new life. It . . . will last forever, for it comes from Christ. . . . Our natural lives will fade as grass. . . All our greatness is like a flower that droops and falls."
1 Peter 1:23,24

Peter wrote to strengthen the Christians in what is now Turkey because of coming persecution and trials. In doing so he used vivid images they would appreciate: seedtime and harvest, flocks and shepherds, 'waterless springs and mists driven by a storm'.

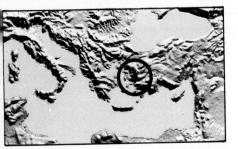

Smyrna

*"Write down everything you see, and send
your letter to the seven churches in
Turkey: to the church in Ephesus, the
one in Smyrna, and those in Pergamos,
Thyatira, Sardis, Philadelphia and Laodicea.
Stop being afraid of what you are about to
suffer—for the devil will soon throw
some of you into prison to test you."*
Revelation 1:11; 2:10

The aged apostle John was exiled on the
island of Patmos. The book of Revelation
was written mainly in the literary form of
apocalyptic, possibly to disguise its anti-
Roman content, certainly because its
rich imagery was the only way to convey
his vision of the lordship of Christ in
history. The first part is a series of letters
to seven churches on the mainland, in
the order in which a messenger would
have reached them. Smyrna is today the
busy industrial seaport city of Izmir. The
Forum, pictured here, is the chief
evidence of its Roman past.

Pergamum

"I am . . . aware that you live . . . where Satan's throne is. . . ." Revelation 2:13

On a great rocky acropolis overlooking the small Turkish town of Bergama are the remains of the ancient town of Pergamum. Behind the theatre is the site of the great altar of Zeus. Pergamum was not only a center for the worship of the traditional gods, Zeus, Dionysus and Athena, but the place where the worship of the Roman Emperor first took hold.

Temple dedicated to the Emperor Trajan.

Away from the main acropolis of Pergamum is the ruin of a Temple of Asclepius, the god of healing. Under the floor were water conduits; behind the arch is the end of a tunnel which may have been used for some sort of shock therapy for nervous disease. Medical treatment was mixed with mystery religion: its pagan immorality may underlie some of the references in John's letter.

149

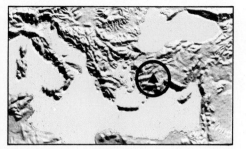

Laodicea

"I know you well—you are neither hot nor cold; I wish you were one or the other! But since you are merely lukewarm, I will spit you out of my mouth!"
Revelation 3:15,16

A few miles from Laodicea are the hot springs of Hierapolis. The two towns were mentioned together by Paul in his letter to Colossae, also nearby. The water was channelled along conduits to Laodicea itself—and would have arrived tepid.

Mineral deposits from the water onto the conduits have made them solid and permanent.

The waters from Hierapolis flow over cliffs: over the centuries the mineral deposits have built up into terraces and lime 'waterfalls'.

From the site of Laodicea itself the white cliffs of Hierapolis can be seen in the distance. Laodicea was also a commercial center for banking and the wool trade, and a medical center: gold, clothing and eye-salve are all alluded to in John's letter.

Judgment and glory

" 'Alas, alas, for that great city! . . .
in a single hour all is gone. . . .'
But you, O heaven, rejoice over her fate;
and you, O children of God and the prophets
and the apostles! For at last God has
given judgment against her for you. . . .
'Praise the Lord. For the Lord our God,
the Almighty, reigns. Let us be glad and
rejoice and honor him. . . .' "
Revelation 18:19,20; 19:6,7

Revelation was written against the
background of persecution and
martyrdom, to encourage endurance to
the end. It also looked to a time when
even the persecuting Roman Empire itself
would pass, when Christ and his faithful
followers would be vindicated; when there
would be new heavens and a new earth.